Heart on Fire For God

60- Day Devotional

DR. SONYA ALISE MCKINZIE

Table of Contents

Dedication

This devotional is dedicated to all those who seek strength, hope, and love in their daily lives. May these reflections and prayers inspire you to draw closer to God and find peace in His presence. Whether you are facing challenges, celebrating joys, or simply seeking a deeper connection with your faith, may this devotional be a source of comfort and guidance.

To the weary, may you find rest.
To the hopeful, may you find fulfillment.
To the loving, may you find joy.

May God's grace and love surround you always.

Acknowledgements

To my family and friends, your unwavering support and encouragement have been invaluable. To my spiritual mentors, thank you for your wisdom and guidance, which have deeply influenced these reflections.

A special thanks to the community of believers who inspire me daily with their faith and love. Your stories and experiences have enriched this devotional and made it a true labor of love.

Above all, I thank God for His endless grace and love, which have been the foundation of this work. May this devotional bring comfort, strength, and inspiration to all who read it.

Embracing Self-Love

Scripture:

"Love your neighbor as yourself." - Mark 12:31 (NIV)

Reflection:

In this verse, Jesus emphasizes the importance of loving others, but it also implies that we must first love ourselves. Self-love is not about vanity or selfishness; it's about recognizing our worth as creations of God. When we love ourselves, we acknowledge that we are fearfully and wonderfully made (Psalm 139:14). This self-acceptance allows us to extend genuine love and compassion to others.

Prayer:

Dear Lord, help me to see myself through Your eyes. Teach me to appreciate the unique qualities You've given me and to treat myself with kindness and respect. May I find strength in Your love and use it to uplift others. Amen.

Action Step:

Take a moment today to write down three things you appreciate about yourself. Reflect on these qualities and thank God for making you who you are. Let this practice remind you of your inherent worth and inspire you to love others more deeply.

Finding Hope in Depression

Scripture:
"The Lord is close to the brokenhearted and saves those who are crushed in spirit." - Psalm 34:18 (NIV)

Reflection:
Depression can feel like a heavy burden, isolating us from the world and even from God. Yet, the Bible reassures us that God is near to those who are suffering. He understands our pain and offers comfort and hope. In moments of deep despair, we can turn to Him, knowing that He is our refuge and strength (Psalm 46:1). It's important to remember that seeking help from others, whether through friends, family, or professional support, is also a way God provides for us.

Prayer:
Heavenly Father, I come to You in my time of need. Please lift the weight of depression from my heart and mind. Surround me with Your love and peace. Help me to feel Your presence and to trust in Your healing power. Amen.

Action Step:
Reach out to someone you trust and share your feelings. Sometimes, simply talking about what you're going through can bring relief. Consider seeking professional help if needed. Remember, it's okay to ask for help.

Strengthening Your Faith

Scripture:
"Now faith is confidence in what we hope for and assurance about what we do not see." - Hebrews 11:1 (NIV)

Reflection:
Faith is the cornerstone of our relationship with God. It is believing in His promises even when we cannot see the outcome. Faith gives us the strength to face challenges, knowing that God is in control. It is through faith that we find peace in uncertainty and courage in adversity. Remember, faith is not about having all the answers but trusting that God does. As we grow in faith, we learn to rely more on His wisdom and less on our understanding (Proverbs 3:5-6).

Prayer:
Lord, increase my faith. Help me to trust in Your plans for my life, even when I cannot see the way forward. Give me the courage to step out in faith, knowing that You are with me every step of the way. Strengthen my belief in Your promises and help me to live a life that reflects Your love and grace. Amen.

Action Step:
Take a moment to reflect on a time when your faith was tested. How did you see God working in that situation? Write down your thoughts and thank God for His faithfulness. Let this reflection remind you of His constant presence and encourage you to trust Him more deeply.

Facing Your Goliaths

Scripture:
"David said to the Philistine, 'You come against me with sword and spear and javelin, but I come against you in the name of the Lord Almighty, the God of the armies of Israel, whom you have defied.'" - 1 Samuel 17:45 (NIV)

Reflection:
We all face "Goliaths" in our lives—those seemingly insurmountable challenges that test our faith and strength. David's encounter with Goliath teaches us that no matter how daunting our hardships may seem, we can overcome them with God's help. David did not rely on his own strength but trusted in God's power and faithfulness. When we face our own giants, we can draw courage from David's example, knowing that God is with us and will fight for us.

Prayer:
Lord, I bring my struggles before You. Just as You gave David the courage to face Goliath, grant me the strength to confront my own challenges. Help me to trust in Your power and not be overwhelmed by fear. Remind me that with You, all things are possible. Amen.

Action Step:
Identify a "Goliath" in your life—a hardship or challenge that you are currently facing. Write it down and pray over it, asking God for the strength and wisdom to overcome it. Reflect on past victories where God has helped you, and let these memories bolster your faith.

Cherishing Family

Scripture:
"Behold, how good and how pleasant it is for brethren to dwell together in unity!" - Psalm 133:1 (KJV)

Reflection:
Family is one of God's greatest gifts to us. It is within the family that we first experience love, support, and a sense of belonging. The Bible emphasizes the importance of family unity and harmony. When we cherish and nurture our family relationships, we reflect God's love and create a strong foundation for our lives. Just as God loves us unconditionally, we are called to love and support our family members, forgiving their shortcomings and celebrating their strengths.

Prayer:
Heavenly Father, thank You for the gift of family. Help me to appreciate and cherish my loved ones. Teach me to be patient, kind, and forgiving, just as You are with me. Strengthen our bonds and guide us to live in harmony and love. Amen.

Action Step:
Take time today to express your love and appreciation to each family member. Whether through a kind word, a thoughtful gesture, or spending quality time together, let them know how much they mean to you. Reflect on the ways you can contribute to a loving and supportive family environment.

The Parenting Journey

Scripture:
"Train up a child in the way he should go, and when he is old, he will not depart from it." - Proverbs 22:6 (NKJV)

Reflection:
Parenting is one of the most rewarding yet challenging roles we can undertake. It requires patience, wisdom, and unconditional love. The Bible provides guidance on how to raise children in a way that honors God. Proverbs 22:6 reminds us of the importance of instilling values and faith in our children from a young age. As parents, we are called to be role models, showing our children the love of Christ through our actions and words. Remember, we are not alone in this journey—God is with us, providing strength and guidance.

Prayer:
Dear Lord, thank You for the blessing of children. Help me to be a loving and wise parent, guiding my children in Your ways. Give me patience and understanding and help me to reflect Your love in all that I do. May my children grow to know and love You deeply. Amen.

Action Step:
Spend intentional time with your children today. Whether it's through a shared activity, a meaningful conversation, or simply being present, let them know they are valued and loved. Use this time to teach them about God's love and to reinforce positive values.

Deepening My Prayer Life

Scripture:
"Devote yourselves to prayer, being watchful and thankful." - Colossians 4:2 (NIV)

Reflection:
Prayer is our direct line of communication with God. It is through prayer that we express our gratitude, seek guidance, and find comfort. Strengthening our prayer life involves making it a consistent and heartfelt practice. By devoting ourselves to prayer, we become more attuned to God's presence and His will for our lives. Remember, prayer is not just about asking for things; it's about building a relationship with God, listening to His voice, and aligning our hearts with His.

Prayer:
Lord, help me to deepen my prayer life. Teach me to come to You with a thankful heart, to seek Your guidance, and to listen for Your voice. Strengthen my faith and help me to trust in Your plans. May my prayers reflect my love and devotion to You. Amen.

Action Step:
Set aside a specific time each day for prayer. Create a quiet space where you can focus on connecting with God. Start with a few minutes and gradually increase the time as you become more comfortable. Use this time to express your gratitude, share your concerns, and listen for God's guidance.

Finding Peace in Anxiety

Scripture:
"Do not be anxious about anything, but in every situation, by prayer and petition, with thanksgiving, present your requests to God." - Philippians 4:6 (NIV)

Reflection:
Anxiety can feel overwhelming, but God's Word offers us comfort and guidance. Philippians 4:6 encourages us to bring our worries to God through prayer. When we do this, we are reminded that we are not alone in our struggles. God cares deeply about our concerns and invites us to cast all our anxieties on Him (1 Peter 5:7). By focusing on His promises and expressing gratitude, we can find peace even amid anxiety.

Prayer:
Heavenly Father, I come to You with my anxieties and fears. Help me to trust in Your love and care. Teach me to bring my worries to You in prayer and to find peace in Your presence. Thank You for Your constant support and for the assurance that You are always with me. Amen.

Action Step:
Take a few moments today to write down your anxieties. Then, pray over each one, asking God to help you release these worries into His hands. Reflect on the things you are grateful for and thank God for His blessings.

Nurturing Your Marriage

Scripture:
"Above all, love each other deeply, because love covers over a multitude of sins." - 1 Peter 4:8 (NIV)

Reflection:
Marriage is a sacred covenant that reflects God's love for us. It requires commitment, patience, and a deep, abiding love. In 1 Peter 4:8, we are reminded to love each other deeply, understanding that love can overcome many challenges. A strong marriage is built on mutual respect, open communication, and a willingness to forgive. By prioritizing our relationship with our spouse and seeking God's guidance, we can nurture a marriage that honors Him and brings joy to our lives.

Prayer:
Lord, thank You for the gift of marriage. Help us to love each other deeply and to support one another through all of life's challenges. Teach us to communicate openly and to forgive quickly. May our marriage reflect Your love and grace. Amen.

Action Step:
Spend quality time with your spouse today. Whether it's a heartfelt conversation, a shared activity, or simply enjoying each other's company, try to connect and strengthen your bond. Reflect on the ways you can show love and appreciation to your spouse.

Embracing Abstinence

Scripture:
"Flee from sexual immorality. All other sins a person commits are outside the body, but whoever sins sexually, sins against their own body." - 1 Corinthians 6:18 (NIV)

Reflection:
Abstinence is a commitment to purity and self-control, honoring God with our bodies and our choices. In a world that often promotes instant gratification, choosing abstinence can be challenging, but it is a powerful way to demonstrate our faith and dedication to God's will. By abstaining from sexual immorality, we protect our hearts and minds, allowing us to grow closer to God and to prepare ourselves for a future relationship that is grounded in love and respect. Remember, our bodies are temples of the Holy Spirit (1 Corinthians 6:19-20), and we are called to honor God with them.

Prayer:
Lord, help me to honor You with my body and my choices. Give me the strength to remain pure and to resist temptation. Guide me in my journey of abstinence and help me to find fulfillment in Your love and purpose for my life. Amen.

Action Step:
Reflect on your reasons for choosing abstinence and write them down. Keep this list as a reminder of your commitment and as a source of strength when you face challenges. Surround yourself with supportive friends and mentors who share your values and can encourage you in your journey.

Finding Comfort in Grief

Scripture:
"Blessed are those who mourn, for they will be comforted." - Matthew 5:4 (NIV)

Reflection:
Grief is a profound and personal experience that can leave us feeling lost and overwhelmed. In times of mourning, it is important to remember that God is with us, offering comfort and peace. Jesus' words in Matthew 5:4 remind us that those who grieve are blessed because they will receive God's comfort. Grief is a journey, and while it may never fully go away, God's presence can bring healing and hope. Lean on Him and allow His love to surround you during this difficult time.

Prayer:
Heavenly Father, I come to You with a heavy heart. Please comfort me in my grief and help me to feel Your presence. Give me the strength to face each day and the hope to see beyond my sorrow. Surround me with Your love and peace. Amen.

Action Step:
Take time to honor your feelings and memories. Whether through journaling, talking with a trusted friend, or creating a memorial, find a way to express your grief. Allow yourself to mourn and seek support from those around you.

Overcoming Racism with Love

Scripture:
"There is neither Jew nor Gentile, neither slave nor free, nor is there male and female, for you are all one in Christ Jesus." - Galatians 3:28 (NIV)

Reflection:
Racism is a sin that divides and harms individuals and communities. The Bible teaches us that in Christ, we are all equal and united. Galatians 3:28 reminds us that our identity in Christ transcends all earthly distinctions. As followers of Jesus, we are called to love one another and to stand against injustice. Overcoming racism requires us to see each person as made in the image of God and to treat them with dignity and respect. By promoting love, understanding, and equality, we can help build a world that reflects God's kingdom.

Prayer:
Lord, help me to see others as You see them. Give me the courage to stand against racism and to promote love and equality. Teach me to love my neighbor as myself and to work towards justice and reconciliation. May my actions reflect Your love and grace. Amen.

Action Step:
Educate yourself about the experiences and histories of different racial and ethnic groups. Engage in conversations about race with humility and openness. Seek ways to support and uplift those who are marginalized and to advocate for justice in your community.

Seeking God's Guidance in Your Career

Scripture:
"Commit to the Lord whatever you do, and he will establish your plans." - Proverbs 16:3 (NIV)

Reflection:
Our careers are an important part of our lives, providing not only for our needs but also offering opportunities to serve others and glorify God. Proverbs 16:3 reminds us to commit our work to the Lord, trusting that He will guide and establish our plans. Whether you are just starting out, seeking a new direction, or striving to grow in your current role, it's essential to seek God's wisdom and guidance. By aligning our career goals with His will, we can find fulfillment and purpose in our work.

Prayer:
Lord, I commit my career to You. Guide my steps and give me wisdom in my decisions. Help me to use my talents and opportunities to serve others and to honor You. May my work reflect Your love and grace. Amen.

Action Step:
Take time to reflect on your career goals and aspirations. Write them down and pray over them, asking God for guidance and clarity. Consider how your work can serve others and bring glory to God. Seek counsel from trusted mentors or colleagues who share your faith.

Strength in the Journey with PCOS

Scripture:
"I can do all this through him who gives me strength." - Philippians 4:13 (NIV)

Reflection:
Living with Polycystic Ovary Syndrome (PCOS) can be challenging, both physically and emotionally. It can affect many aspects of life, from health to self-esteem. However, Philippians 4:13 reminds us that we can find strength in Christ to face any challenge. God understands our struggles and is with us every step of the way. By leaning on His strength, we can navigate the difficulties of PCOS with hope and resilience. Remember, you are not alone in this journey—God's love and support are always with you.

Prayer:
Dear Lord, I come to You with my struggles and concerns about PCOS. Please give me the strength and courage to face each day. Help me to trust in Your plan for my life and to find comfort in Your presence. Guide me to the right resources and support and help me to take care of my body and mind. Amen.

Action Step:
Take time to educate yourself about PCOS and seek support from healthcare professionals, support groups, or loved ones. Practice self-care by maintaining a healthy lifestyle, including balanced nutrition, regular exercise, and stress management. Reflect on the ways God has provided strength and comfort in your life and thank Him for His constant presence.

Heart on Fire for God

Scripture:
"Never be lacking in zeal, but keep your spiritual fervor, serving the Lord." - Romans 12:11 (NIV)

Reflection:
Being "on fire for God" means having a passionate and enthusiastic relationship with Him. It's about maintaining a fervent spirit and a deep desire to serve and honor God in all aspects of our lives. Romans 12:11 encourages us to keep our spiritual fervor alive, reminding us that our zeal for God should be evident in our actions and attitudes. This kind of passion can inspire others and draw them closer to God. To stay on fire for God, we need to nurture our faith through prayer, worship, and studying His Word, allowing His love to fuel our hearts.

Prayer:
Lord, ignite a fire in my heart for You. Help me to maintain my zeal and passion for serving You. Fill me with Your Spirit and guide me in living a life that reflects Your love and grace. May my enthusiasm for You inspire others and bring glory to Your name. Amen.

Action Step:
Dedicate time each day to deepen your relationship with God. This could be through prayer, reading the Bible, worship, or serving others. Reflect on what ignites your passion for God and seek to incorporate those activities into your daily routine. Share your faith and enthusiasm with others, encouraging them to also seek a deeper relationship with God.

The Gift of Friendship

Scripture:
"A friend loves at all times, and a brother is born for a time of adversity." - Proverbs 17:17 (NIV)

Reflection:
Friendship is a precious gift from God, providing us with companionship, support, and joy. True friends love us unconditionally and stand by us through life's ups and downs. Proverbs 17:17 highlights the enduring nature of genuine friendship, reminding us that friends are there for us in times of need. As we cherish our friendships, we should strive to be the kind of friend who reflects God's love—loyal, compassionate, and encouraging. By nurturing our friendships, we create a network of support that strengthens our faith and enriches our lives.

Prayer:
Lord, thank You for the gift of friendship. Help me to be a loving and supportive friend, reflecting Your love in my relationships. Teach me to appreciate and nurture the friends You have placed in my life. May our friendships bring glory to You and strengthen our faith. Amen.

Action Step:
Reach out to a friend today and express your gratitude for their presence in your life. Whether through a heartfelt message, a phone call, or spending time together, let them know how much they mean to you. Reflect on ways you can be a better friend and support those around you.

Finding Healing After Divorce

Scripture:
"The Lord is close to the brokenhearted and saves those who are crushed in spirit." - Psalm 34:18 (NIV)

Reflection:
Divorce is a painful and challenging experience that can leave us feeling broken and alone. However, God's Word assures us that He is close to the brokenhearted and offers healing and comfort. Psalm 34:18 reminds us that God is present in our pain and is ready to save and restore us. During this difficult time, it's important to lean on God's strength and seek His guidance. He understands our struggles and promises to walk with us through every trial. By trusting in His love and grace, we can find hope and begin the journey toward healing.

Prayer:
Heavenly Father, I come to You with a heavy heart. Please comfort me in my pain and help me to find healing and peace. Guide me through this difficult time and give me the strength to move forward. Surround me with Your love and support and help me to trust in Your plan for my life. Amen.

Action Step:
Take time to care for yourself emotionally and spiritually. Seek support from trusted friends, family, or a counselor. Spend time in prayer and reflection, asking God to heal your heart and guide your steps. Remember that healing is a process, and it's okay to take it one day at a time.

Overcoming Trials & Tribulations

Scripture:
"I can do all this through him who gives me strength." - Philippians 4:13 (NIV)

Reflection:
Life is filled with obstacles that can test our faith and resilience. Whether they are personal challenges, professional setbacks, or spiritual struggles, these obstacles can feel overwhelming. However, Philippians 4:13 reminds us that we can overcome any challenge through Christ who strengthens us. God equips us with the strength and courage we need to face our difficulties. By trusting in His power and leaning on His promises, we can navigate through life's obstacles with confidence and hope.

Prayer:
Lord, I bring my challenges before You. Please give me the strength and wisdom to overcome them. Help me to trust in Your power and to rely on Your guidance. Remind me that with You, all things are possible. Strengthen my faith and help me to see obstacles as opportunities for growth. Amen.

Action Step:
Identify an obstacle you are currently facing. Write it down and pray over it, asking God for the strength and guidance to overcome it. Reflect on past challenges where God has helped you, and let these memories encourage you. Take practical steps towards addressing the obstacle, trusting that God is with you every step of the way.

Spiritual Warfare and God's Armor

Scripture:
"Put on the full armor of God, so that you can take your stand against the devil's schemes." - Ephesians 6:11 (NIV)

Reflection:
Spiritual warfare is a reality for every believer. The Bible teaches us that we are in a battle not against flesh and blood, but against spiritual forces of evil (Ephesians 6:12). To stand firm in this battle, we must equip ourselves with the full armor of God. This includes the belt of truth, the breastplate of righteousness, the gospel of peace, the shield of faith, the helmet of salvation, and the sword of the Spirit, which is the Word of God (Ephesians 6:13-17). By relying on God's strength and protection, we can face any spiritual attack with confidence and victory.

Prayer:
Lord, I acknowledge the spiritual battles I face. Help me to put on Your full armor each day. Strengthen my faith and protect me from the enemy's schemes. Guide me in Your truth and righteousness and fill me with Your peace. May Your Word be my weapon and Your salvation my shield. Amen.

Action Step:
Take time to study Ephesians 6:10-18 and reflect on each piece of God's armor. Consider how you can apply these spiritual tools in your daily life. Pray for God's protection and strength as you face spiritual challenges. Stay connected to a community of believers who can support and encourage you in your spiritual journey.

Finding Freedom from Alcoholism

Scripture:
"So if the Son sets you free, you will be free indeed." - John 8:36 (NIV)

Reflection:
Overcoming alcoholism is a challenging journey that requires strength, support, and faith. John 8:36 reminds us that true freedom comes through Jesus Christ. He offers us the power to break free from the chains of addiction and to live a life of purpose and peace. Recovery is not just about abstaining from alcohol; it's about finding healing and transformation through God's love and grace. By leaning on Him and seeking His guidance, we can find the strength to overcome addiction and to embrace a new, healthier way of living.

Prayer:
Lord, I come to You seeking freedom from alcoholism. Please give me the strength and courage to overcome this addiction. Surround me with supportive people and resources that can help me on this journey. Fill me with Your peace and guide me towards a life of health and wholeness. Thank You for Your unfailing love and for the freedom You offer. Amen.

Action Step:
Reach out for support from trusted friends, family, or a support group. Consider seeking professional help if needed. Create a plan for your recovery that includes prayer, accountability, and healthy habits. Reflect on the ways God has already worked in your life and thank Him for His continued presence and guidance.

Breaking the Chains of Drug Addiction

Scripture:
"Therefore, if anyone is in Christ, the new creation has come: The old has gone, the new is here!" - 2 Corinthians 5:17 (NIV)

Reflection:
Overcoming drug addiction is a difficult and often painful journey, but it is one that can lead to profound transformation and renewal. 2 Corinthians 5:17 reminds us that in Christ, we are made new. This promise of new life and freedom is available to all who seek it. Recovery from addiction involves not only breaking free from physical dependence but also finding healing for the mind and spirit. By turning to God and relying on His strength, we can experience true freedom and become the new creation He intends us to be.

Prayer:
Lord, I seek Your help in overcoming my addiction. Please give me the strength and courage to break free from this bondage. Surround me with supportive people and resources that can guide me on this path to recovery. Help me to trust in Your power to transform my life and to embrace the new creation You have made me to be. Amen.

Action Step:
Reach out for support from trusted friends, family, or a support group. Consider seeking professional help if needed. Create a plan for your recovery that includes prayer, accountability, and healthy habits. Reflect on the ways God has already worked in your life and thank Him for His continued presence and guidance.

Finding Confidence in God's Love

Scripture:
"I praise you because I am fearfully and wonderfully made; your works are wonderful; I know that full well." - Psalm 139:14 (NIV)

Reflection:
Insecurity can creep into our lives in many ways, making us doubt our worth and abilities. However, God's Word reminds us that we are fearfully and wonderfully made. Psalm 139:14 speaks to the unique and intentional way God created each of us. When we understand that we are His masterpiece, we can begin to see ourselves through His eyes. Overcoming insecurity involves embracing our identity in Christ and trusting in His love and purpose for our lives. By focusing on God's truth rather than our fears, we can find confidence and peace.

Prayer:
Lord, help me to see myself as You see me. Remove the insecurities that hold me back and fill me with Your love and confidence. Remind me of my worth and purpose in You. Guide me to trust in Your plans and to embrace the person You created me to be. Amen.

Action Step:
Take time to reflect on the qualities and strengths God has given you. Write down affirmations based on Scripture that remind you of your worth and identity in Christ. Whenever you feel insecure, read these affirmations and pray for God's reassurance.

Healing From Abuse

Scripture:
"The Lord is close to the brokenhearted and saves those who are crushed in spirit." - Psalm 34:18 (NIV)

Reflection:
Experiencing abuse can leave deep emotional and physical scars, making it difficult to trust and feel safe. However, God's Word assures us that He is close to the brokenhearted and offers healing and comfort. Psalm 34:18 reminds us that God sees our pain and is present with us in our suffering. Healing from abuse is a journey that requires time, support, and faith. By leaning on God's love and seeking His guidance, we can find the strength to overcome the past and move towards a future filled with hope and peace.

Prayer:
Heavenly Father, I come to You with my pain and brokenness. Please heal my heart and mind from the wounds of abuse. Surround me with Your love and comfort and guide me towards healing and restoration. Help me to trust in Your plan for my life and to find peace in Your presence. Amen.

Action Step:
Seek support from trusted friends, family, or a counselor who can help you navigate the healing process. Spend time in prayer and reflection, asking God to guide you and to bring peace to your heart. Consider joining a support group where you can share your experiences and find encouragement from others who have faced similar challenges.

Striving to Thrive in God's Grace

Scripture:
"I have come that they may have life and have it to the full." - John 10:10 (NIV)

Reflection:
God's desire for us is not just to survive but to thrive. Jesus came so that we might have life to the fullest, experiencing His joy, peace, and purpose. Thriving means growing in our faith, using our gifts to serve others, and living out our God-given potential. It involves embracing the abundant life that Jesus offers and trusting in His plans for us. By seeking God's guidance and relying on His strength, we can move beyond mere existence and truly flourish in every aspect of our lives.

Prayer:
Lord, help me to thrive in Your grace. Show me how to live a life that is full and abundant, reflecting Your love and purpose. Guide me to grow in my faith and to use my gifts to serve others. May my life be a testament to Your goodness and grace. Amen.

Action Step:
Identify areas in your life where you feel you are merely surviving rather than thriving. Pray for God's guidance and take practical steps to improve these areas. This might include setting new goals, seeking mentorship, or dedicating more time to spiritual growth. Trust that God will lead you towards a life of abundance and fulfillment.

Loving Others as Christ Loves Us

Scripture:
"A new command I give you: Love one another. As I have loved you, so you must love one another." - John 13:34 (NIV)

Reflection:
Jesus calls us to love others as He loves us—unconditionally, sacrificially, and without judgment. This kind of love goes beyond mere feelings; it is an active choice to care for and serve others. Loving others means showing kindness, compassion, and forgiveness, even when it is difficult. It involves putting others' needs before our own and seeking their well-being. By loving others as Christ loves us, we reflect His love to the world and fulfill His commandment.

Prayer:
Lord, help me to love others as You love me. Teach me to show kindness, compassion, and forgiveness in all my relationships. Give me the strength to love even when it is challenging. May my actions reflect Your love and bring glory to Your name. Amen.

Action Step:
Think of someone in your life who could use a reminder of God's love. Reach out to them with a kind gesture, a word of encouragement, or an act of service. Reflect on how you can show love to others in your daily interactions and make a conscious effort to do so.

Embracing Grace Over Judgment

Scripture:
"Do not judge, or you too will be judged." - Matthew 7:1 (NIV)

Reflection:
Judging others can be an easy trap to fall into, but Jesus teaches us to refrain from judgment. Matthew 7:1 reminds us that the measure we use to judge others will be used against us. Instead of focusing on others' faults, we are called to extend grace and understanding. By recognizing our own imperfections and the grace God has shown us, we can approach others with compassion rather than criticism. Embracing grace over judgment helps us build stronger, more loving relationships and reflects the heart of Christ.

Prayer:
Lord, help me to see others through Your eyes. Teach me to extend grace and understanding instead of judgment. Remind me of the grace You have shown me and help me to reflect that same grace to those around me. May my actions and words be filled with love and compassion. Amen.

Action Step:
The next time you find yourself tempted to judge someone, pause and pray for them instead. Reflect on your own need for grace and how you can show kindness and understanding. Make a conscious effort to speak and act with compassion in your interactions.

Honoring Mothers

Scripture:
"Her children arise and call her blessed; her husband also, and he praises her: 'Many women do noble things, but you surpass them all.'" - Proverbs 31:28-29 (NIV)

Reflection:
Mothers hold a special place in our hearts and lives. They are often the backbone of the family, providing love, support, and guidance. Proverbs 31 celebrates the virtues of a godly woman, highlighting the strength, wisdom, and compassion that mothers embody. Honoring our mothers means recognizing their sacrifices and expressing our gratitude for their unwavering love. It also involves supporting and encouraging them in their journey. By appreciating and valuing our mothers, we reflect God's love and honor His commandment to respect our parents.

Prayer:
Lord, thank You for the gift of mothers. Bless them with strength, wisdom, and joy. Help us to honor and appreciate them every day. Give us the words and actions to express our gratitude and love. May our relationships with our mothers be filled with Your grace and peace. Amen.

Action Step:
Take time today to show appreciation for your mother or a mother figure in your life. Whether through a heartfelt message, a thoughtful gift, or spending quality time together, let her know how much she means to you. Reflect on the ways she has impacted your life and thank God for her presence.

Embracing Life Changes

Scripture:
"There is a time for everything, and a season for every activity under the heavens." - Ecclesiastes 3:1 (NIV)

Reflection:
Life is full of changes, some expected and others surprising. Ecclesiastes 3:1 reminds us that there is a season for everything, and each change we experience is part of God's plan. Embracing change can be challenging, but it also offers opportunities for growth and renewal. By trusting in God's timing and His purpose for our lives, we can navigate transitions with faith and confidence. Remember, God is with us in every season, guiding us and providing the strength we need to adapt and thrive.

Prayer:
Lord, help me to embrace the changes in my life with faith and trust in Your plan. Give me the strength to adapt and the wisdom to see the opportunities for growth. Remind me that You are with me in every season, guiding and supporting me. May I find peace in Your presence and confidence in Your purpose. Amen.

Action Step:
Reflect on a recent change in your life. Consider how this change has impacted you and what you have learned from it. Write down your thoughts and pray for God's guidance and strength as you continue to navigate this transition. Seek support from friends, family, or a faith community to help you through this season.

Spirituality vs Religion

Scripture:
"God is spirit, and his worshipers must worship in the Spirit and in truth." -
John 4:24 (NIV)

Reflection:
The terms "spirituality" and "religion" are often used interchangeably, but they can have different meanings. Religion typically refers to organized practices and beliefs shared by a community, while spirituality is more about an individual's personal relationship with God. Both have their place in our faith journey. Religion provides structure, community, and tradition, helping us to grow in our faith alongside others. Spirituality, on the other hand, emphasizes a personal connection with God, fostering an intimate and direct relationship with Him. True worship involves both—engaging in communal practices while also nurturing our personal spiritual life. By balancing both aspects, we can deepen our faith and live out our beliefs more fully.

Prayer:
Lord, help me to find the balance between spirituality and religion in my life. Guide me to engage meaningfully in my faith community while also nurturing my personal relationship with You. Teach me to worship You in spirit and in truth, and to grow in my faith both individually and collectively. Amen.

Action Step:
Reflect on your own faith journey. Consider how you engage with both religious practices and personal spirituality. Identify areas where you can deepen your involvement in your faith community and ways to enhance your personal spiritual practices. Plan to incorporate both aspects into your daily life.

Compassion

Scripture Reading:*"Be kind and compassionate to one another, forgiving each other, just as in Christ God forgave you.*Ephesians 4:32 (NIV)

Reflection: Compassion is a profound and powerful expression of love. It goes beyond mere sympathy and involves a deep empathy for others, coupled with a desire to alleviate their suffering. Jesus exemplified compassion throughout His ministry, healing the sick, feeding the hungry, and comforting the broken-hearted.

Meditation: Take a moment to reflect on the times when you have experienced compassion from others. How did it make you feel? Now, think about how you can extend that same compassion to those around you. Compassion doesn't always require grand gestures; sometimes, a simple act of kindness can make a significant difference in someone's life.

Prayer: Heavenly Father, thank You for the boundless compassion You have shown us through Jesus Christ. Help us to be vessels of Your love and compassion in this world. Open our eyes to the needs of those around us and give us the courage to act with kindness and empathy. May our actions reflect Your love and bring comfort to those who are hurting. Amen.

Action Step: This week, make a conscious effort to show compassion in your daily interactions. Whether it's offering a listening ear, helping a neighbor, or simply smiling at a stranger, let your actions be a testament to the love and compassion of Christ.

Walking in Empathy

Scripture Reading: *"Rejoice with those who rejoice; mourn with those who mourn."* - Romans 12:15 (NIV)

Reflection: Empathy is the ability to understand and share the feelings of another. It is a vital aspect of our relationships and a key component of living out our faith. Jesus demonstrated empathy in His interactions, showing deep understanding and compassion for the struggles and joys of those He encountered.

Meditation: Consider a time when someone truly understood what you were going through. How did their empathy impact you? Reflect on how you can be more empathetic in your daily life. Empathy involves listening without judgment, being present, and offering support without trying to fix everything.

Prayer: Lord, thank You for the gift of empathy. Help us to be more like Jesus, who showed perfect empathy in His love for us. Open our hearts to the experiences of others and give us the grace to walk alongside them in their joys and sorrows. Teach us to listen with compassion and respond with kindness. Amen.

Action Step: This week, practice empathy by actively listening to someone without interrupting or offering solutions. Simply be present and show that you care. Your willingness to understand and share in their experience can be a powerful source of comfort and connection.

Overcoming Imposter Syndrome

Scripture Reading:*"For we are God's handiwork, created in Christ Jesus to do good works, which God prepared in advance for us to do."* - Ephesians 2:10 (NIV)

Reflection: Imposter syndrome is the feeling of being inadequate despite evident success. Many of us struggle with this, doubting our abilities and fearing that we will be exposed as frauds. However, the Bible reminds us that we are God's handiwork, uniquely created and equipped for the good works He has planned for us.

Meditation: Reflect on the times when you have felt like an imposter. What triggered those feelings? Now, consider the truth of God's Word: you are fearfully and wonderfully made (Psalm 139:14). God has given you unique gifts and talents for a purpose. Embrace your identity in Christ and trust in His plan for your life.

Prayer: Heavenly Father, thank You for creating us with purpose and intention. Help us to see ourselves through Your eyes and to overcome the doubts that make us feel like imposters. Strengthen our faith in Your promises and remind us of our worth in You. May we walk confidently in the path You have set before us. Amen.

Action Step: This week, whenever you feel like an imposter, take a moment to affirm your identity in Christ. Write down a list of your God-given strengths and accomplishments. Reflect on how God has used you in the past and trust that He will continue to work through you.

Finding Light in Seasonal Affective Disorder (SAD)

Scripture Reading: *"The light shines in the darkness, and the darkness has not overcome it."* - John 1:5 (NIV)

Reflection: Seasonal Affective Disorder (SAD) is a type of depression that occurs at certain times of the year, usually in the winter when daylight hours are shorter. It can bring feelings of sadness, fatigue, and hopelessness. However, the Bible reminds us that even in the darkest times, the light of Christ shines brightly and cannot be overcome.

Meditation: Think about a time when you felt overwhelmed by darkness, whether physically or emotionally. How did you find your way back to the light? Reflect on the ways God has been a source of light and hope in your life. Remember that His light is always present, even when it feels hidden.

Prayer: Lord, we thank You for being our light in the darkness. When we face the challenges of SAD or any form of depression, help us to remember that Your light is always with us. Give us the strength to seek help and the courage to reach out to others. Fill our hearts with Your hope and peace. Amen.

Action Step: This week, plan to incorporate more light into your daily routine. Spend time outside during daylight hours, even if it's just for a short walk. Reach out to a friend or family member for support. Consider starting a gratitude journal to focus on the positive aspects of each day.

Nurturing Mental Health

Reflection: Mental health is a crucial aspect of our overall well-being, yet it is often overlooked or stigmatized. The Bible encourages us to bring our worries and anxieties to God, reminding us that He cares deeply for us. Acknowledging our mental health struggles and seeking help is a sign of strength, not weakness.

Meditation: Reflect on a time when you felt overwhelmed by stress or anxiety. How did you cope with those feelings? Consider how turning to God in prayer and seeking support from others can provide relief and comfort. Remember that God is always with you, offering His peace and understanding.

Prayer: Heavenly Father, thank You for Your constant presence in our lives. We lift up our mental health struggles to You, knowing that You care for us deeply. Grant us the courage to seek help when we need it and the wisdom to support others in their times of need. Fill us with Your peace and guide us towards healing and wholeness. Amen.

Action Step: This week, take a proactive step towards nurturing your mental health. This could be setting aside time for prayer and meditation, talking to a trusted friend or counselor, or engaging in activities that bring you joy and relaxation. Remember, taking care of your mental health is an important part of honoring the body and mind God has given you.

Physical Health

Scripture Reading: *"Do you not know that your bodies are temples of the Holy Spirit, who is in you, whom you have received from God? You are not your own; you were bought at a price. Therefore, honor God with your bodies."* - 1 Corinthians 6:19-20 (NIV)

Reflection: Our physical health is a gift from God, and taking care of our bodies is an act of worship. Just as we nurture our spiritual health through prayer and reading Scripture, we should also be mindful of our physical well-being. This includes eating nutritious foods, exercising regularly, and getting adequate rest.

Meditation: Think about how you currently care for your body. Are there areas where you could improve? Reflect on the connection between your physical health and your spiritual well-being. Consider how making healthier choices can enhance your ability to serve God and others.

Prayer: Lord, thank You for the gift of our bodies and the ability to care for them. Help us to see our physical health as an important part of our spiritual journey. Give us the discipline to make healthy choices and the strength to maintain them. May our actions honor You and reflect our gratitude for the bodies You have given us. Amen.

Action Step: This week, set a specific goal to improve your physical

health. It could be as simple as drinking more water, taking a daily walk, or incorporating more fruits and vegetables into your diet. Remember that small, consistent changes can lead to significant improvements over time.

Understanding True Prosperity

Scripture Reading: *"Beloved, I pray that you may prosper in all things and be in health, just as your soul prospers."* 3 John 1:2 (NKJV)

Reflection: Prosperity is often associated with material wealth and success, but true prosperity encompasses much more. It includes spiritual, emotional, and physical well-being. God desires for us to prosper in all areas of our lives, aligning our hearts with His will and purpose.

Meditation: Reflect on what prosperity means to you. Is it solely about financial success, or does it include other aspects of your life? Consider how your relationship with God influences your understanding of prosperity. True prosperity is found in a life that is rich in faith, love, and purpose.

Prayer: Heavenly Father, thank You for Your desire for us to prosper in all things. Help us to seek true prosperity that aligns with Your will. Teach us to value spiritual growth and emotional well-being as much as material blessings. May our lives reflect Your abundance and grace. Amen.

Action Step: This week, focus on an area of your life where you seek greater prosperity. It could be deepening your spiritual practices, nurturing relationships, or taking steps towards better health. Trust that God will guide you towards true prosperity as you align your actions with His will.

Overcoming Odds

Scripture Reading: *"I can do all things through Christ who strengthens me."* - Philippians 4:13 (NKJV)

Reflection: Life often presents us with challenges that seem insurmountable. Whether it's personal struggles, health issues, or external obstacles, we can feel overwhelmed and defeated. However, the Bible reminds us that with Christ, we have the strength to overcome any odds. His power is made perfect in our weakness, and through Him, we can achieve what seems impossible.

Meditation: Think about a time when you faced significant odds. How did you respond? Reflect on how God's presence and strength helped you through that situation. Remember that no matter how daunting the challenge, God is with you, providing the strength and courage you need.

Prayer: Lord, thank You for being our source of strength and courage. When we face overwhelming odds, remind us that we can do all things through Christ who strengthens us. Help us to trust in Your power and lean on Your promises. Give us the perseverance to keep moving forward, knowing that You are with us every step of the way. Amen.

Action Step: This week, identify a challenge you are currently facing. Write down a plan to tackle it, including steps you can take and ways you can rely on God's strength. Share your plan with a trusted friend or family member for support and accountability.

Embracing Your God-Given Identity

Scripture Reading: *"For we are God's masterpiece. He has created us anew in Christ Jesus, so we can do the good things He planned for us long ago."* - Ephesians 2:10 (NLT)

Reflection: Understanding and embracing who God made us to be is a journey of faith and self-discovery. We are often our own harshest critics, focusing on our flaws and shortcomings. However, God sees us as His masterpiece, uniquely crafted with purpose and intention. Recognizing our worth in His eyes can transform how we view ourselves and our place in the world.

Meditation: Take a moment to reflect on the qualities and talents that make you unique. How do these reflect God's handiwork in your life? Consider the ways in which you can use your gifts to serve others and fulfill the purpose God has for you. Embrace the truth that you are fearfully and wonderfully made (Psalm 139:14).

Prayer: Heavenly Father, thank You for creating us with love and purpose. Help us to see ourselves through Your eyes and to embrace our identity in Christ. Remove the doubts and insecurities that cloud our vision and fill us with confidence in Your perfect design. Guide us to use our gifts for Your glory and to live out the calling You have placed on our lives. Amen.

Action Step: This week, write down a list of your strengths and positive qualities. Reflect on how these attributes can be used to serve God and others. Share this list with a trusted friend or mentor who can encourage you and help you see yourself as God does.

God's Grace and Mercy

Scripture Reading:*"The Lord is compassionate and gracious, slow to anger, abounding in love. He will not always accuse, nor will He harbor His anger forever; He does not treat us as our sins deserve or repay us according to our iniquities."* Psalm 103:8-10 (NIV)

Reflection: God's grace and mercy are two of His most profound gifts to us. Grace is the unmerited favor that God bestows upon us, while mercy is His compassion and forgiveness towards us, even when we deserve punishment. Together, they reveal the depth of God's love and His desire for us to live in freedom and joy.

Meditation: Reflect on a time when you experienced God's grace and mercy in your life. How did it change your perspective or actions? Consider how you can extend that same grace and mercy to others. Remember that God's love for you is unconditional and everlasting, and He continually offers you His grace and mercy.

Prayer: Heavenly Father, thank You for Your boundless grace and mercy. We are humbled by Your love and forgiveness, which we do not deserve but gratefully receive. Help us to live in the light of Your grace, extending mercy to others as You have shown it to us. May our lives be a testament to Your incredible love and compassion. Amen.

Action Step: This week, practice extending grace and mercy in your interactions. When someone wrongs you, choose forgiveness over resentment. When you see someone in need, offer help without expecting anything in return. Let your actions reflect the grace and mercy that God has shown you.

Experiencing God's Unfailing Love

Scripture Reading: *"For I am convinced that neither death nor life, neither angels nor demons, neither the present nor the future, nor any powers, neither height nor depth, nor anything else in all creation, will be able to separate us from the love of God that is in Christ Jesus our Lord.* Romans 8:38-39 (NIV)

Reflection: God's love for us is immeasurable and unconditional. It is a love that surpasses all understanding and remains constant through every circumstance. This love was most profoundly demonstrated through the sacrifice of Jesus Christ, who gave His life so that we might be reconciled with God. No matter what we face, we can rest in the assurance that God's love is always with us.

Meditation: Take a moment to reflect on the ways you have experienced God's love in your life. How has His love comforted you in times of trouble or brought joy in moments of happiness? Consider how you can share this love with others, reflecting God's heart in your daily interactions.

Prayer: Heavenly Father, thank You for Your unfailing love. We are grateful for the assurance that nothing can separate us from Your love. Help us to live in the light of this truth, sharing Your love with those around us. May our lives be a testament to Your incredible love and grace. Amen.

Action Step: This week, make a conscious effort to show love to those around you. Whether it's through a kind word, a helping hand, or simply being present for someone in need, let your actions reflect the love of God. Remember that even small acts of love can have a profound impact.

Selflessness

Scripture Reading: *"Do nothing out of selfish ambition or vain conceit. Rather, in humility value others above yourselves, not looking to your own interests but each of you to the interests of the others."* - Philippians 2:3-4 (NIV)

Reflection: Selflessness is at the heart of the Christian faith. Jesus exemplified the ultimate act of selflessness by sacrificing His life for our salvation. We are called to follow His example by putting the needs of others before our own and serving them with humility and love. True selflessness is not about neglecting our own needs but about finding joy in lifting others up.

Meditation: Reflect on a time when you put someone else's needs before your own. How did it make you feel? Consider the impact of your actions on that person. Think about ways you can practice selflessness in your daily life, whether through small acts of kindness or more significant sacrifices.

Prayer: Lord, thank You for the perfect example of selflessness You have given us in Jesus. Help us to cultivate a heart of humility and to value others above ourselves. Give us the strength to serve selflessly and the wisdom to know how best to support those around us. May our actions reflect Your love and bring glory to Your name. Amen.

Action Step: This week, look for opportunities to practice selflessness. It could be as simple as helping a colleague with a task, volunteering your time, or offering a listening ear to someone in need. Let your actions be motivated by love and a genuine desire to serve others.

Cultivating Inner Beauty

Scripture Reading: *"Your beauty should not come from outward adornment, such as elaborate hairstyles and the wearing of gold jewelry or fine clothes. Rather, it should be that of your inner self, the unfading beauty of a gentle and quiet spirit, which is of great worth in God's sight."* - 1 Peter 3:3-4 (NIV)

Reflection: In a world that often emphasizes outward appearance, it's important to remember that true beauty comes from within. Inner beauty is characterized by qualities such as kindness, compassion, humility, and a gentle spirit. These attributes reflect the heart of Christ and are of great value in God's eyes. Cultivating inner beauty involves nurturing our relationship with God and allowing His love to transform us from the inside out.

Prayer: Heavenly Father, thank You for reminding us that true beauty comes from within. Help us to cultivate inner beauty by nurturing our relationship with You and developing qualities that reflect Your love. Teach us to value what You value and to seek beauty that is unfading and eternal. May our lives reflect Your grace and goodness. Amen.

Action Step: This week, focus on one aspect of inner beauty that you would like to develop. It could be practicing patience, showing kindness, or being more compassionate. Make a conscious effort to embody this quality in your interactions with others and ask God to help you grow in this area.

Trusting God without Doubt

Scripture Reading: *"Trust in the Lord with all your heart and lean not on your own understanding; in all your ways submit to Him, and He will make your paths straight."* - Proverbs 3:5-6 (NIV)

Reflection: Doubt is a natural part of the human experience, but it can hinder our relationship with God and our ability to fully trust in His plans. The Bible encourages us to trust in the Lord with all our heart, even when we don't understand His ways. By surrendering our doubts and leaning on God's wisdom, we can find peace and assurance in His perfect plan for our lives.

Meditation: Think about a time when you struggled with doubt. How did it affect your relationship with God and your decision-making? Reflect on the ways God has been faithful in your life, even when things didn't make sense. Consider how you can strengthen your trust in Him and let go of your doubts.

Prayer: Heavenly Father, thank You for Your unwavering faithfulness. Help us to trust in You with all our hearts and to surrender our doubts to You. Give us the courage to lean on Your understanding and not our own. Strengthen our faith and guide us in Your perfect ways. May we find peace in knowing that You are always in control. Amen.

Action Step: This week, identify an area of your life where you are struggling with doubt. Write down a prayer of surrender, giving that doubt to God and asking for His guidance and peace. Reflect on His promises and remind yourself of His faithfulness.

Full Healing

Scripture Reading: *"He heals the brokenhearted and binds up their wounds."* - Psalm 147:3 (NIV)

Reflection: Full healing encompasses not just physical restoration but also emotional, mental, and spiritual wholeness. God is our ultimate healer, capable of mending our deepest wounds and restoring us to complete health. Whether we are dealing with physical ailments, emotional scars, or spiritual struggles, we can trust in God's power to heal us fully.

Meditation: Reflect on an area of your life where you need healing. It could be a physical condition, an emotional hurt, or a spiritual struggle. Consider how God's healing touch has already worked in your life and how He continues to offer His healing power. Trust that He is with you in every step of your healing journey.

Prayer: Heavenly Father, thank You for being our healer. We come to You with our brokenness, knowing that You have the power to restore us completely. Heal our bodies, minds, and spirits, and help us to trust in Your perfect timing and plan. May we experience the fullness of Your healing and live in the wholeness that You desire for us. Amen.

Action Step: This week, take a step towards healing in an area of your life. It could be seeking medical help, talking to a counselor, spending time in prayer and meditation, or reaching out to a trusted friend for support. Remember that healing is a process, and God is with you every step of the way.

Jesus, Our Everything

Scripture Reading:*"And my God will meet all your needs according to the riches of His glory in Christ Jesus."* Philippians 4:19 (NIV)

Reflection: Jesus is our everything. He is our Savior, our Redeemer, our Friend, and our Provider. In Him, we find all that we need for life and godliness. When we place our trust in Jesus, we can rest assured that He will meet all our needs according to His glorious riches. He is the source of our strength, our peace, and our joy.

Meditation: Reflect on the ways Jesus has been your everything. How has He provided for you, comforted you, and guided you? Consider the areas of your life where you need to rely more fully on Him. Trust that Jesus is sufficient for every need and that His love and grace are more than enough.

Prayer: Lord Jesus, thank You for being our everything. We are grateful for Your constant presence and provision in our lives. Help us to rely on You fully and to trust in Your sufficiency. May we find our strength, peace, and joy in You alone. Guide us in all that we do and remind us daily of Your unfailing love. Amen.

Action Step: This week, make a conscious effort to turn to Jesus in every situation. Whether you are facing a challenge or celebrating a victory, acknowledge His presence and rely on His strength. Spend time in prayer and worship, focusing on His sufficiency and thanking Him for being your everything.

The Sacrifice of Jesus

Scripture Reading:*"But God demonstrates His own love for us in this: While we were still sinners, Christ died for us.*Romans 5:8 (NIV)

Reflection: The death of Jesus on the cross is the ultimate demonstration of God's love for us. Jesus willingly gave His life to pay the penalty for our sins, offering us the gift of salvation and eternal life. This sacrificial love is the foundation of our faith and the source of our hope. Through His death and resurrection, Jesus conquered sin and death, providing a way for us to be reconciled with God.

Meditation: Reflect on the significance of Jesus' sacrifice. How does His death on the cross impact your life and faith? Consider the depth of His love and the magnitude of His sacrifice. Let this reflection deepen your gratitude and commitment to living a life that honors Him.

Prayer: Lord Jesus, thank You for Your incredible sacrifice on the cross. We are humbled by the depth of Your love and the price You paid for our salvation. Help us to live in a way that reflects our gratitude for Your sacrifice. Strengthen our faith and guide us to share Your love with others. Amen.

Action Step: This week, take time to meditate on the story of Jesus' crucifixion and resurrection. Read the accounts in the Gospels and reflect on what His sacrifice means for you personally. Share this message of love and hope with someone who may need to hear it.

Sabbath Day

Scripture Reading: *"Remember the Sabbath day by keeping it holy. Six days you shall labor and do all your work, but the seventh day is a sabbath to the Lord your God. On it you shall not do any work, neither you, nor your son or daughter, nor your male or female servant, nor your animals, nor any foreigner residing in your towns."* Exodus 20:8-10 (NIV)

Reflection: The Sabbath day is a gift from God, a time set apart for rest and spiritual renewal. It is a day to cease from our labors and focus on our relationship with God. Observing the Sabbath allows us to recharge physically, mentally, and spiritually, and to remember that our worth is not based on our productivity but on our identity as God's beloved children.

Meditation: Reflect on how you currently observe the Sabbath. Do you take time to rest and focus on God, or do you find it difficult to set aside your work and responsibilities? Consider the benefits of honoring the Sabbath and how it can deepen your relationship with God and improve your overall well-being.

Prayer: Heavenly Father, thank You for the gift of the Sabbath. Help us to honor this day by setting aside our work and focusing on You. Teach us to find rest in Your presence and to trust in Your provision. May our observance of the Sabbath bring us closer to You and renew our spirits. Amen.

Action Step: This week, plan to observe the Sabbath. Set aside time for rest, worship, and reflection. Avoid work and activities that distract you from focusing on God. Use this time to connect with Him through prayer, reading Scripture, and spending time with loved ones.

Celebrating the True Meaning of Christmas

Scripture Reading:*"For unto us a child is born, unto us a son is given, and the government will be upon His shoulder. And His name will be called Wonderful, Counselor, Mighty God, Everlasting Father, Prince of Peace."* Isaiah 9:6 (NKJV)

Reflection: Christmas is a time of joy and celebration, marking the birth of Jesus Christ, our Savior. It is a season to reflect on the incredible gift of God's love and the fulfillment of His promise to send a Redeemer. Amidst the festivities and traditions, it's important to remember the true meaning of Christmas: the arrival of Emmanuel, God with us.

Meditation: Take a moment to reflect on the significance of Jesus' birth. How does His coming into the world impact your life and faith? Consider the ways you can keep Christ at the center of your Christmas celebrations. Let the joy of His birth fill your heart and inspire you to share His love with others.

Prayer: Heavenly Father, thank You for the gift of Your Son, Jesus Christ. As we celebrate His birth, help us to remember the true meaning of Christmas. Fill our hearts with joy and gratitude for Your incredible love. May our celebrations honor You and reflect the light of Christ to those around us. Amen.

Action Step: This Christmas season, find ways to focus on the true meaning of the holiday. Read the nativity story from the Gospels, participate in a Christmas Eve service, or spend time in prayer and reflection. Consider how you can share the love of Christ with others, whether through acts of kindness, giving to those in need, or simply spending quality time with loved ones.

Celebrating Our Differences

Scripture Reading: *"There is neither Jew nor Gentile, neither slave nor free, nor is there male and female, for you are all one in Christ Jesus."* - Galatians 3:28 (NIV)

Reflection: God created each of us uniquely, with different gifts, backgrounds, and perspectives. These differences are not meant to divide us but to enrich our lives and communities. In Christ, we are united body, each part valuable and essential. Celebrating our differences allows us to appreciate the fullness of God's creation and to learn from one another.

Prayer: Heavenly Father, thank You for the beautiful diversity of Your creation. Help us to see each person as You see them, with love and respect. Teach us to celebrate our differences and to learn from one another. Unite us in Your love and help us to build a community that reflects Your kingdom. Amen.

Action Step: This week, try to connect with someone who is different from you. It could be someone from a different cultural background, age group, or with different interests. Take the time to listen to their story and appreciate their unique perspective. Find ways to celebrate and learn from the diversity around you.

Faith Through Struggles

Scripture Reading:*"Consider it pure joy, my brothers and sisters, whenever you face trials of many kinds, because you know that the testing of your faith produces perseverance.*James 1:2-3 (NIV)

Reflection: Struggles are an inevitable part of life, but they also provide opportunities for growth and deeper faith. When we face challenges, it can be difficult to see beyond our immediate pain and frustration. However, the Bible encourages us to view our trials to strengthen our faith and develop perseverance. Trusting in God's plan, even when we don't understand it, allows us to find hope and resilience during our struggles.

Meditation: Think about a recent struggle you have faced. How did it impact your faith? Reflect on how God has been present in your life during difficult times. Consider how your faith has grown through these experiences and how you can continue to trust in God's plan, even when the path is unclear.

Prayer: Heavenly Father, thank You for being with us in our struggles.

Help us to see our trials as opportunities to grow in faith and perseverance. Give us the strength to trust in Your plan and the courage to face our challenges with hope. Remind us that You are always with us, guiding us through every difficulty. Amen.

Action Step: This week, identify a specific struggle you are currently

facing. Write down a prayer of surrender, giving this struggle to God and asking for His guidance and strength. Reflect on His promises and remind yourself of His faithfulness. Share your journey with a trusted friend or mentor who can support you in prayer.

Cleanliness

Scripture Reading: *"Create in me a pure heart, O God, and renew a steadfast spirit within me."* Psalm 51:10 (NIV)

Reflection: Cleanliness is often associated with physical hygiene and tidiness, but it also has a deeper spiritual significance. In the Bible, cleanliness is a metaphor for purity of heart and mind. God desires for us to live lives that are clean and pure, free from sin and filled with His righteousness. Embracing cleanliness in all aspects of our lives can help us draw closer to God and reflect His holiness.

Meditation: Reflect on the areas of your life where you can embrace greater cleanliness, both physically and spiritually. Consider how maintaining a clean and orderly environment can impact your mental and emotional well-being. Think about the importance of having a pure heart and mind, and how you can seek God's help in achieving this.

Prayer: Heavenly Father, thank You for the gift of cleanliness and the

reminder of its importance in our lives. Help us to maintain clean and orderly surroundings, and more importantly, to seek purity of heart and mind. Cleanse us from sin and renew our spirits, so that we may live lives that honor You. Amen.

Action Step: This week, take a step towards greater cleanliness in your life. It could be organizing your living space, practicing good hygiene, or spending time in prayer and reflection to cleanse your heart and mind. Let these actions be a reminder of the importance of purity and order in your spiritual journey.

A Woman's Virtue

Scripture Reading:*"She is clothed with strength and dignity; she can laugh at the days to come.* Proverbs 31:25 (NIV)

Reflection: A woman's virtue reflects her inner strength, dignity, and faith. Proverbs 31 provides a beautiful description of a virtuous woman, highlighting qualities such as wisdom, kindness, and industriousness. These virtues are not just about outward actions but stem from a heart that is aligned with God's will. Embracing these virtues allows women to live out their faith in meaningful and impactful ways.

Meditation: Reflect on the virtues that you see in yourself and in the women around you. How do these qualities reflect God's character? Consider how you can cultivate virtues such as strength, dignity, wisdom, and kindness in your own life. Embrace the unique ways God has equipped you to live out these virtues.

Prayer: Heavenly Father, thank You for the example of the virtuous woman in Proverbs 31. Help us to cultivate these virtues in our own lives, reflecting Your strength, dignity, and wisdom. Teach us to live with kindness and to use our gifts to serve others. May our lives be a testament to Your love and grace. Amen.

Action Step: This week, focus on developing one specific virtue in your

life. It could be practicing kindness, seeking wisdom, or embracing strength and dignity in challenging situations. Look for opportunities to live out this virtue in your interactions with others and in your daily activities.

Cultivating a Heart of Appreciation

Scripture Reading: *"Give thanks in all circumstances; for this is God's will for you in Christ Jesus."* 1 Thessalonians 5:18 (NIV)

Reflection: Appreciation is a powerful practice that can transform our perspective and deepen our relationship with God and others. When we cultivate a heart of appreciation, we recognize the blessings in our lives and express gratitude for them. This attitude of thankfulness aligns us with God's will and helps us to see His hand at work in every situation, both good and challenging.

Meditation: Reflect on the things you are grateful for in your life. How does expressing appreciation impact your mood and outlook? Consider how you can make appreciation a regular part of your daily routine. Think about the people in your life who have been a blessing to you and how you can show your gratitude to them.

Prayer: Heavenly Father, thank You for the many blessings You have given us. Help us to cultivate a heart of appreciation, recognizing Your goodness in every circumstance. Teach us to express our gratitude to You and to those around us. May our lives be filled with thankfulness and joy, reflecting Your love and grace. Amen.

Action Step: This week, make a list of things you are thankful for each day. Take time to thank God for these blessings in your prayers. Additionally, express your appreciation to at least one person each day, whether through a kind word, a note, or an act of kindness. Let your gratitude be a source of encouragement and joy to others.

The Power of Gathering to Help Others

Scripture Reading:*"And let us consider how we may spur one another on toward love and good deeds, not giving up meeting together, as some are in the habit of doing, but encouraging one another—and all the more as you see the Day approaching."*Hebrews 10:24-25 (NIV)

Reflection: Gathering to help others is a powerful expression of our faith and love. When we come together as a community, we can achieve so much more than we could alone. The Bible encourages us to meet regularly, to encourage one another, and to spur each other on toward love and good deeds. By working together, we can make a significant impact in the lives of those in need and reflect the love of Christ to the world.

Prayer: Heavenly Father, thank You for the gift of community and the power of gathering to help others. Help us to see the needs around us and to respond with love and compassion. Teach us to work together, encouraging and supporting one another as we serve. May our collective efforts bring glory to Your name and make a difference in the lives of those we help. Amen.

Action Step: This week, organize or participate in a group activity aimed at helping others. It could be volunteering at a local charity, organizing a food drive, or simply gathering with friends to support a neighbor in need. Encourage others to join you and experience the joy of serving tog

Birthing Prayers

Scripture Reading: *"The prayer of a righteous person is powerful and effective."* - James 5:16b (NIV)

Reflection: Birthing prayers is about bringing forth heartfelt, sincere prayers that come from the depths of our souls. Just as the process of childbirth brings new life into the world, our prayers can bring new hope, healing, and transformation. When we pray with faith and fervor, we align ourselves with God's will and invite His power into our lives and the lives of others.

Meditation: Reflect on the times when you have prayed with deep sincerity and passion. How did those prayers impact your life or the lives of others? Consider the importance of being persistent and earnest in your prayer life. Think about how you can cultivate a deeper, more intimate relationship with God through prayer.

Prayer: Heavenly Father, thank You for the gift of prayer and the opportunity to communicate with You. Help us to birth prayers that are sincere and powerful, aligning with Your will. Teach us to pray with faith and persistence, trusting in Your timing and Your plans. May our prayers bring forth new hope, healing, and transformation in our lives and the lives of those we pray for. Amen.

Action Step: This week, dedicate time each day to pray deeply and sincerely. Focus on specific areas where you seek God's intervention and guidance. Write down your prayers and revisit them, noting how God responds over time. Share your prayer journey with a trusted friend or prayer partner for mutual encouragement and support.

Finding Happiness in God's Love

Scripture Reading: *"The Lord your God is with you, the Mighty Warrior who saves. He will take great delight in you; in His love He will no longer rebuke you but will rejoice over you with singing.* Zephaniah 3:17 (NIV)

Reflection: True happiness is found in the love of God. His love is constant, unconditional, and transformative. When we understand and embrace God's love for us, we can experience a deep and abiding joy that transcends our circumstances. This happiness is not dependent on external factors but is rooted in the assurance that we are loved and cherished by our Creator.

Meditation: Reflect on the ways you have experienced God's love in your life. How does His love bring you happiness and peace? Consider how you can deepen your awareness of His love and let it fill your heart with joy. Remember that God's love is always with you, even in difficult times.

Prayer: Heavenly Father, thank You for Your incredible love that brings true happiness to our lives. Help us to embrace Your love fully and to find joy in Your presence. Teach us to rely on Your love in all circumstances and to share this joy with others. May our lives reflect Your love and happiness. Amen.

Action Step: This week, focus on cultivating happiness through your relationship with God. Spend time in prayer and worship, thanking Him for His love. Look for ways to share His love with others, whether through acts of kindness, words of encouragement, or simply being present for someone in need. Let the joy of God's love shine through you.

Fortitude

Scripture Reading: *"Be strong and courageous. Do not be afraid; do not be discouraged, for the Lord your God will be with you wherever you go."* - Joshua 1:9 (NIV)

Reflection: Fortitude is the strength of mind and spirit that enables us to face adversity with courage and resilience. It is a vital quality for enduring life's challenges and remaining steadfast in our faith. The Bible is filled with examples of individuals who demonstrated fortitude, trusting in God's presence and promises even in the most difficult circumstances. By embracing fortitude, we can navigate our trials with confidence, knowing that God is with us every step of the way.

Meditation: Reflect on a time when you needed fortitude to overcome a challenge. How did your faith help you through that situation? Consider how you can cultivate greater fortitude in your life. Think about the promises of God that give you strength and courage, and how you can rely on them in times of difficulty.

Prayer: Heavenly Father, thank You for being our source of strength and courage. Help us to embrace fortitude in our lives, trusting in Your presence and promises. Give us the resilience to face our challenges with confidence and the faith to remain steadfast in Your love. May we find comfort in knowing that You are always with us, guiding and supporting us through every trial. Amen.

Action Step: This week, identify an area of your life where you need to demonstrate fortitude. Write down a specific challenge you are facing and a Bible verse that encourages you to be strong and courageous. Reflect on this verse daily and ask God for the strength to persevere. Share your journey with a trusted friend or mentor who can support you in prayer.

The Power of Love

Scripture Reading:
"And now these three remain: faith, hope and love. But the greatest of these is love."
— 1 Corinthians 13:13 (NIV)

Reflection:
Love is the cornerstone of our faith and the essence of God's nature. It is through love that we experience the fullness of life and the depth of our relationships. The Apostle Paul, in his letter to the Corinthians, emphasizes that love surpasses all other virtues. It is patient, kind, and enduring. Love is not just an emotion but a deliberate choice to act with compassion and selflessness.

Prayer:
Dear Lord,
Fill my heart with Your love so that I may reflect it in my actions and words. Help me to love others as You have loved me, with patience, kindness, and grace. May Your love be the guiding force in my life, leading me to serve and uplift those around me. Amen.

Action Step:
Think of someone in your life who could use a reminder of love today. Reach out to them with a kind word, a thoughtful g

Deepening My Prayer Life

Scripture:
"Devote yourselves to prayer, being watchful and thankful." - Colossians 4:2 (NIV)

Reflection:
Prayer is our direct line of communication with God. It is through prayer that we express our gratitude, seek guidance, and find comfort. Strengthening our prayer life involves making it a consistent and heartfelt practice. By devoting ourselves to prayer, we become more attuned to God's presence and His will for our lives. Remember, prayer is not just about asking for things; it's about building a relationship with God, listening to His voice, and aligning our hearts with His.

Prayer:
Lord, help me to deepen my prayer life. Teach me to come to You with a thankful heart, to seek Your guidance, and to listen for Your voice. Strengthen my faith and help me to trust in Your plans. May my prayers reflect my love and devotion to You. Amen.

Action Step:
Set aside a specific time each day for prayer. Create a quiet space where you can focus on connecting with God. Start with a few minutes and gradually increase the time as you become more comfortable. Use this time to express your gratitude, share your concerns, and listen for God's guidance.

Finding Security and Safety in God

Scripture Reading:
"The Lord is my rock, my fortress and my deliverer; my God is my rock, in whom I take refuge, my shield and the horn of my salvation, my stronghold."
— Psalm 18:2 (NIV)

Reflection:
In a world filled with uncertainties and dangers, the need for security and safety is paramount. The Bible reassures us that true security is found in God. He is our rock and fortress, a place of refuge where we can find peace and protection. King David, who faced numerous threats and adversities, often spoke of God as his stronghold. This imagery reminds us that no matter what challenges we face, we can trust in God's unwavering protection and care.

Prayer:
Heavenly Father,
Thank You for being my rock and fortress. In times of fear and uncertainty, help me to remember that You are my refuge and strength. Surround me with Your protection and fill my heart with peace. Guide me to trust in Your promises and find safety in Your presence. Amen.

Action Step:
Reflect on areas of your life where you feel vulnerable or anxious. Take a moment to pray and ask God to be your shield and protector in those areas. Consider writing down a verse or affirmation about God's protection and place it somewhere you can see daily as a reminder of His constant care.

Embracing Our Gifts

Scripture Reading:
"We have different gifts, according to the grace given to each of us. If your gift is prophesying, then prophesy in accordance with your faith; if it is serving, then serve; if it is teaching, then teach."
— Romans 12:6-7 (NIV)

Reflection:
Each of us has been blessed with unique gifts and talents, bestowed upon us by God's grace. These gifts are not just for our benefit but are meant to be shared with others, to build up the community and glorify God. The Apostle Paul encourages us to recognize and use our gifts faithfully and joyfully. Whether our gift is teaching, serving, encouraging, or leading, each one is valuable and has a purpose in God's plan.

Prayer:
Gracious God,
Thank You for the unique gifts You have given me. Help me to recognize and develop these gifts, and to use them in ways that honor You and bless others. Give me the courage to step out in faith and share my talents, knowing that You have equipped me for a purpose. Amen.

Action Step:
Take some time to reflect on the gifts and talents you possess. How can you use them to serve others and glorify God? Consider volunteering in your community, church, or a local organization where your gifts can make a positive impact. Write down a plan to put your gifts into action this week.

About the Author

Dr. Sonya Alise McKinzie is a dedicated advocate, author, and educator with a profound commitment to empowering survivors of domestic violence and trauma. Born and raised in Brunswick, GA, Dr. McKinzie has transformed her personal experiences of overcoming domestic violence, PTSD, and anxiety into a mission to support and uplift others.

As the Founder and Executive Director of ThriveHER Incorporated (formerly Women of Virtue Transitional Foundation), established in 2016, Dr. McKinzie has been a beacon of hope and resilience. Her organization focuses on raising awareness about domestic violence and providing support to survivors through various empowerment programs and services.

Dr. McKinzie's academic journey is a testament to her dedication to personal growth and education. She holds degrees in Business Administration, Business Management, and Human Services Counseling, with minors in Addictions & Recovery. She has also earned multiple certifications in fields such as Victims Advocacy, Corporate Leadership and Management, and Human Resources.

In recognition of her tireless efforts and impact, Dr. McKinzie was awarded an honorary doctorate in Humanitarianism in 2024. She is also a certified trauma and recovery life coach and a prominent figure in the Marsy's Law Movement, advocating for victims' rights.

Dr. McKinzie is the author of 28 books, primarily focusing on healing and navigating the aftermath of abuse and trauma. Her writings and advocacy work continue to inspire and empower individuals to break free from the cycle of abuse and lead fulfilling lives.

Through her unwavering faith and dedication, Dr. Sonya Alise McKinzie exemplifies the power of resilience and the transformative impact of love and support.